REFLECTIVE SUPERVISION TOOLKIT

Daphne Hewson and Michael Carroll

Companion volume to
Reflective Practice in Supervision

Published by MoshPit Publishing, an imprint of
Mosher's Business Support Pty Ltd
PO Box 147
Hazelbrook NSW 2779
www.indiemosh.com.au

The moral right of the authors has been asserted in accordance with the *Copyright Amendment (Moral Rights) Act* 2000.

Cataloguing-in-Publication entry is available from the National Library of Australia: http://catalogue.nla.gov.au/

Title:
Reflective Supervision Toolkit

Authors:
Hewson, Daphne
Carroll, Michael

ISBN:
978-1-925529-78-4 (paperback)

Cover design by Katya Shmaiger kaligraphicprint.com.au

Cover photo represents 'Negative capability':
Being in uncertainties, mysteries, doubts,
without any irritable reaching after fact and reason
(Keats)

Photo credits
Cover: Eugene May/Shutterstock.com/7447678
Cellar inside back cover: FooTToo/Shutterstock.com/256178800
Manager's Office inside back cover: greatpapa/Shutterstock.com/23803408
Exam Room and Sitting Room on back cover: Louise Cousins
Office on back cover: Lane V Erickson/Shutterstock.com/271099724
Observatory on back cover (Mont Blanc): Alison Saxton

CONTENTS

ABOUT THIS TOOLKIT

This toolkit is for use in conjunction with our book *Reflective Practice in Supervision*. We've printed it as a separate volume to provide a format that's easy to use in supervision. The tools do not stand alone. We present them on the assumption that you've read the book sufficiently to understand the principles and risks of reflective supervision.

The book and toolkit are based on our belief that reflection is at the heart of supervision. Yes, there are other tasks in supervision (we present five other supervisory spaces; p. 6) but for us, reflection is what makes supervision supervision. We define reflection as "mindful consideration" and see reflection in supervision as comprising three stances: the Mindful Stance (pause, notice, mark), the Consideration Stance (explore, unearth assumptions and make meaning) and the Consolidation Stance (integrating new learning into practice).

As discussed in *Reflective Practice in Supervision*, tools are often criticised in the literature as superficial recipes. While acknowledging that reflective tools can be misused and overused, we've found them to be very helpful for learning the complex process of reflective practice. Remember the story from Minuchin and Fishman (1981) that we quoted near the start of the book:

> *The training of the samurai was a training in spontaneity... To become a master, he had to train as a warrior for three to five years. Then, having become a craftsman, he was required to abandon his craft and spend a number of years studying unrelated areas, like painting, poetry, or calligraphy. Only after achieving mastery in these different intellectual endeavours could a warrior go back and take up the sword, for only then had the sword become a continuation of the arm. He had become a samurai because he had forgotten technique. This, clearly, is the meaning given to the concept of the spontaneous therapist.*

This toolkit provides you with the techniques you'll forget when you become a spontaneous reflective practitioner. Think of learning to drive a car. At first, you need to be shown which pedal to press and which gear to choose for various conditions and then you need to practise these skills over and over to become proficient in their use. After a while you don't think of pedals and gears and mirrors – you become a spontaneous driver.

The tools introduce you to a range of approaches to reflective practice. The goal is for you to master the techniques and then discard the tools as you develop reflective skills.

The tools might appear to be simple lists of questions, but this apparent simplicity is deceptive! They can elicit deep and meaningful reflections in a very short time and it is not uncommon for strong emotional reactions ("the growing edge" (Berger, 2004), Chapter E3 in *Reflective Practice in Supervision*), to be part of the reflective experience.

The Tools

Following the cooking metaphor that we used in *Reflective Practice in Supervision*, this toolkit includes both mini-tools (the ingredients of reflective practice) and tools (some full recipes). Mini-tools are one-liners, taken from E2 (Noticing mini-tools), E4 (Consideration mini-tools) and E6 (Consolidation mini-tools). We suggest you choose a few that interest you and try using them. Write them on the Key Mini-tools page at the end of the toolkit so they are easily accessible. Over time you'll gain a sense of where they fit and how they work. When you've become familiar with them, choose others to add to your mini-toolkit.

The full tools involve a time commitment. Some can be done in 15 minutes or so (e.g. Values), but most take 30 to 60 minutes. Note also that Jan Fook and Fiona Gardner (2007) recommend having a break of several days or more between the process of unearthing assumptions (Mindful Consideration) and the process of fine-tuning the practice framework and putting the new learning into action (Consolidation). As we discussed in E5, the Consolidation stance is often a cycle process of conceptualisation – practise – reflection – refinement – further practise, to "build the muscle" (Bennett-Levy et al, 2015) of the new learning. So it's beneficial to plan for the Consolidation part of each tool to spread over several sessions to give the practitioner's new learning a chance to be fully incorporated.

To use the tools effectively, you need to choose the right one for a particular purpose at a particular time. This means you need to understand each one sufficiently to be able to judge how well it fits and then to use it skillfully. It's not a matter of reading the questions out like a script. You need to select those that fit the context and the practitioner's changing needs. This takes practice. We suggest starting with one or two tools (perhaps PP and SIS) and developing expertise in those before starting to experiment with other tools. We also suggest that, during the initial learning period, you keep to one tool at a time rather than flicking between them. Once you've mastered numerous tools you'll be able to interweave them with ease. Or drop them altogether and simply use mini-tools or your own reflective questions.

The tools are particularly useful for group supervision (Chapter F3). When group members agree on which tool to use, then everyone is playing the same "piece of music" and the orchestra will sound a lot better than if each person jumps to their preferred piece.

Our tools don't venture into the creative arts. We recommend Lahad (2000) and Schuck and Wood (2011) for many stimulating ideas for creative supervision tools.

As a reminder, we start with a summary of the Principles of reflective practice in supervision. The chapter headings (e.g. F3), refer to chapters in *Reflective Practice in Supervision.* PDF files of some of the forms are available on www.reflectivesupervision.com and demonstration videos of some of the tools are available on YouTube (https://youtu.be/4k4hsog8Ops (capital O not zero) or go to youtube.com and enter Daf Hewson, then search for *Reflective Supervision Toolkit)*

PRINCIPLES OF
REFLECTIVE PRACTICE IN SUPERVISION

Chapter	Principle/Guideline
Part A Supervision and Reflective Practice	
A1 Principles	Keep coming back to the basics
A2 What is supervision?	Focus on the practitioner's learning
A3 What are supervisory spaces?	Check you are both in the supervisory space that fits your current needs
A4 What are helium balloons?	Reflect to ensure you "get it"
A5 What is reflection?	Pause to notice and then consider the meaning of what you noticed
A6 What is reflective practice?	Consolidate new learning into practice and into your practice framework
A7 What is a practice framework?	Aim to fine-tune your practice framework
Part B Reflective Space	
B1 What is reflective space?	S - Safety first P - Trust the process A - Be aware and "out" C - Be curious E - Embrace whatever comes up
B2 What's the "dark side" of reflective supervision?	Acknowledge and monitor the risks of reflective supervision
B3 How is reflective space created?	Co-create reflective space
B4 What environment is needed for reflective supervision?	Prepare an environment that says, "you matter"
B5 What preparation does the practitioner need?	Provide role induction Prepare for supervision
B6 What preparation does the supervisor need?	In reflective space, be a mindful friend
B7 What preparation does the organisation need?	Ensure the organisation understands and supports reflection
B8 What preparation does the relationship need?	Ensure the relationship is "good enough" for the task at hand

PRINCIPLES OF
REFLECTIVE PRACTICE IN SUPERVISION
(continued)

Chapter	Principle/Guideline
Part C Concepts	
C1 How do I reflect on my "other" mind?	Infer the assumptions of the "other mind"
C2 How do frames set problems?	Notice how the problem has been framed
C3 What is critical reflection?	Hunt down and challenge your deepest assumptions
C4 Whose gaze is shaping my work?	Assess shoulds and shouldn'ts in terms of your own values
C5 What do I focus on when I reflect?	Explore as widely as the practitioner is ready for
Part D Feedback	
D1 How can I give better feedback?	Throw catchable feedback balls to someone who is ready, willing and able to catch them
D2 How can I avoid feedback mistakes?	Stay connected
D3 How do I give reflective feedback?	Ask before you tell Shine a light into the darkness and invite reflective dialogue
D4 Is formal feedback useful in supervision?	Seek formal feedback
D5 How do I respond to feedback?	WHAM feedback to get the most out of it

D. Hewson and M. Carroll *Reflective Supervision Toolkit*

PRINCIPLES OF
REFLECTIVE PRACTICE IN SUPERVISION
(continued)

Chapter	Principle/Guideline
Part E Putting Theory into Practice	
E1 What do I do in the Mindful Stance?	Pause and notice
E2 Mini-tools for noticing	Look, look, and look again; there is always more to notice
E3 What do I do in the Consideration Stance?	Embrace uncertainty and be willing to be unsettled
E4 Mini-tools for the Consideration Stance	Hunt for assumptions and unsettle them
E5 What do I do in the Consolidation Stance?	Conceptualise, commit, plan and embody the new learning
E6 Mini-tools for the Consolidation Stance	"Build the muscle" of the new learning
Part F Frequently Asked Questions	
F1 How soon can trainees start reflective practice?	Embrace reflective learning from the start
F2 Isn't evidence-based practice preferable to subjective navel-gazing?	Maintain three stable legs on your practice stool
F3 How does reflective supervision work in a group?	Work together as an orchestra or as in a "jam" session
F4 Why is reflection-in-action so hard to do?	Clarify your practice framework and "support team" ready to draw on them when in-action
F5 How do I deal with problems?	Dancing, not wrestling
F6 Why is it so hard to do reflective supervision?	Engage with your "threshold concepts"

Supervision can be seen as a house with six rooms (A3), each with a different purpose (as shown in the figure on the back cover of this toolkit). The supervisor and practitioner have different roles in each room, and these roles create the different relationships between them. Of course, you don't move between physical rooms during supervision. Each "room" is a relational space and the movement is between different roles. Each relational space both holds and restrains. It holds in the sense that we know who we are to the other and how to be in our role, freeing us to be fully present in that moment. It restrains by delimiting what can happen between us.

All the rooms are built on a common foundation. They share the common goal of learning and the common tasks of monitoring, formative feedback and support. Each room provides a relational space with unique goals and tasks as summarised below.

All the rooms have a useful purpose, but they are not all used in every supervision session. Most supervision happens in the three rooms (Sitting Room, Studio and Observatory) in the bottom row of the figure.

DIRECTIVE SPACE

Room: Office
Primary goals: Safeguard the public and comply with requirements
Supervisor's role: Director (Give directions)
Practitioner's role: Follower (Follow directions)

EVALUATIVE SPACE

Room: Exam Room
Primary goals: Evaluate practitioner's current performance to provide a summative assessment
Supervisor's role: Examiner (Conduct assessment, give feedback)
Practitioner's role: Examinee (Be open to assessment and feedback)

PASSIVE SPACE

Room: Lecture Theatre
Primary goal: Impart information or advice
Supervisor's role: Lecturer/Advisor (Provide information and advice)
Practitioner's role: Student (Learn by listening)

RESTORATIVE SPACE

Room: Sitting Room
Primary goal: Debrief until 'settled'
Supervisor's role: Colleague (Debrief and celebrate)
Practitioner's role: Colleague (Be open to debriefing and celebration)

ACTIVE SPACE

Room: Studio
Primary goal: Collaborative solutions
Supervisor's role: Interactive thinker and learner
(Teaching, learning and problem-solving)
Practitioner's role: Interactive thinker and learner
(Teaching, learning and problem-solving)

REFLECTIVE SPACE

Room: Observatory
Primary goal: Discovery
Supervisor's role: Mindful friend (Support practitioner to reflect)
Practitioner's role: Explorer (Reflect)

NON-SUPERVISORY SPACES

Sometimes the supervisor or practitioner wanders off to rooms that are not supervisory spaces. Two common non-supervisory spaces are shown at the end of this toolkit (p. 62).

MANAGERIAL SPACE When the supervisor has the dual roles of supervisor and manager, they sometimes jump into their managerial role during supervision. One way to reduce this risk is to move physically out of their manager's office and into a different room to conduct supervision and to commit to providing only the six supervisory spaces in the supervision room.

AVOIDANCE SPACE The Cellar is the place where practitioners flee when supervision doesn't seem safe. They hide there and wait for the session to be over. Some supervisors also hide in the Cellar, especially those who resent being landed with supervising when they're already overworked. They chat or complain or find other ways to fill the time. None of these behaviours meets the needs of any of the supervisory spaces.

SELF-CARE GRID

Purpose: To help you to review your self-care practices using Loehr and Schwartz's (2003) four sources of energy: physical, emotional, mental and spiritual.

Stress, burnout, compassion fatigue and vicarious traumatisation are just some of the possible consequences of working in the helping professions.

It is an ethical obligation, not just a personal need, to attend to self-care so that we can remain physically and psychologically healthy and meet the demands of our jobs. One of the supervisor's tasks (restorative) is to support practitioners to care for themselves.

Warning Signs of Occupational Stress [1]

- Loss of pleasure in work
- Depression (sleep or appetite disturbance, lethargy, negative mood)
- Inability to focus or concentrate; forgetfulness
- Anxiety
- Substance use/abuse or other compulsive behaviours
- More frequent clinical errors
- Less contact with colleagues
- "Workaholism"
- Persistent thoughts about clients and their clinical material
- Intrusive imagery from clients' traumatic material
- Increased cynicism, overgeneralised negative beliefs
- Increased isolation from or conflict with intimates
- Chronic irritability, impatience
- Increased reactivity and loss of objective and perspective in work
- Suicidal thoughts.

How to use: Allow lots of time to complete the grid. Then reflect on your self-care practices.
We use the tool SIS (Slogan-Incident-Slogan) to facilitate this reflective process.

Background: Adapted from Loehr and Schwartz (2003)

References: [1]American Psychological Association (2010)

SELF-CARE GRID

	Physically	Emotionally	Mentally	Spiritually
What currently energises me in my work?				
What saps my energy in my work?				
What would help to energise me more in my work?				
What holds me back from doing what would energise me more?				

Some examples of what you might enter into each column:

Physical	Emotional	Mental	Spiritual
Eating	Relationships	Time management	Commitment
Drinking	Intimacy	Creativity	Values
Sleeping	Empathy	Thinking skills	A deeper purpose
Exercise	Processing emotions	Challenge	Prayer/meditation
Breaks	Balance	Mental preparation	Giving to others
Relaxation	Safety	Reflection	Nature
			Stillness

Adapted from Loehr and Schwartz (2003)

SUPERVISION FEEDBACK FORM

Purpose: To provide formal feedback on each supervision session (D4)

How to use: We recommend using the Supervision Feedback Form in every session. This ensures supervision is geared to the practitioner's changing needs and also creates a climate of giving and receiving feedback.

- At the start of the session, ask the practitioner to indicate their current needs on the grid with an X.
- If their rating is unusual or surprising, ask them about what's happening for them.
- During the supervision session, gear the degree of challenge and support to meet their identified need.
- Towards the end of the session, ask the practitioner to mark the grid again with a T (for how today's session went) and then complete the other 4 ratings. This only takes a minute or two.
- At the same time, you could rate each item on how you think the session went for the practitioner.
- WHAM(M) the feedback (D5)
  - Discuss any discrepancy between the practitioner's X and T ratings
  - Discuss the practitioner's ratings (and any discrepancies between practitioner's and supervisor's ratings)
  - Negotiate how to address any difficulties

Note: the feedback is likely to be very positive the first few times this form is used. The test comes when the practitioner makes the first rating that indicates even a slight difficulty. If the supervisor doesn't WHAMM (D5) this feedback well, then they can't expect open and useful feedback in the future.

Background: Formal feedback, known as Feedback Informed Treatment (FIT, Miller, 2011) (D4), improves clinical treatment outcomes (Duncan, Miller, Wampold and Hubble, 2009;; Lambert and Shimokawa, 2011). This form for formal feedback in supervision combines Wainwright's (2010) Leeds Alliance in Supervision Scale with the challenge/support grid from Inskipp and Proctor (1993)

Other references: Duncan, Miller, Sparks et al. (2003), Green and Latchford (2012), Maeschalck et al. (2012), www.scottmiller.com

SUPERVISION FEEDBACK FORM

Names: _____

Date: _____

Before session: please put a mark (X) where you would like today's session to be

HIGH
CHALLENGE

HIGH   LOW
SUPPORT ————————————— SUPPORT

LOW
CHALLENGE

After the session:
- please put a mark (T) on above grid where Today's session was for you and
- put a mark on the lines (below) nearest to the description that best fits your experience.

Approach

This supervision session | This supervision session
was *not* focused ├──────────────────────────┤ was focused

Relationship

My supervisor and I did | My supervisor and I
not understand each ├──────────────────────────┤ understood each other in
other in this session | this session

Meeting my needs

This supervision session | This supervision session
was *not* helpful for me ├──────────────────────────┤ was helpful for me

Combines Inskipp & Proctor's (1993) challenge/support grid with Wainwright's (2010) Leeds Alliance in Supervision Scale (LASS, reproduced with permission of the author).

NOTABLE INCIDENTS

Purpose   To provide a format for preparing for supervision (B5). Sometimes preparation for supervision is left to chance or takes place in a vague, general manner. This format provides a useful first person account of an experience that's helpful for reflective supervision. An example of the use of Pat's notable incident (next page) is given in A5.

Background   This format is derived from Jan Fook and Fiona Gardner. We've changed the term "critical incident" to "notable incident" because practitioners interpret the word "critical" in various ways including "a grave condition", "crucial", "urgent", "criticism" and "critical incident debriefing".

References   Fook and Gardner (2007)

NOTABLE INCIDENT INSTRUCTIONS

1. Choose a notable incident to discuss in supervision. A notable incident is any experience that you regard as noteworthy.
   - It can be something that went well, or something that didn't go so well, or something that you aren't sure about.
   - It is not necessarily a major event or crisis. Experiences that could be described as typical, normal, mundane, or trivial can provide rich material for reflection because many taken-for-granted theories and values are embedded in our routine practices.
   - It is not necessarily big or lengthy. Assumptions are embedded in even the smallest and briefest of notable incidents, and the smaller and less horrific the incident, the safer it is likely to be to reflect on it.
   - Ensure that you feel safe to present it in supervision.
   - Ensure you can present it in an ethical way (e.g. protecting the confidentiality and safety of all others involved).

2. Write a maximum of one page in three sections:

   - **Background** to the incident (very brief)
   - **Incident** A raw and concrete description of the incident
        Focus on one or more moments, not everything that happened
        Use your own words, <u>in first person, present tense</u>
        Don't interpret – just raw description
   - **Significance** Why the incident is notable or significant (the reason could be that it's so routine you think it's time to check it out)

3. Please try NOT to analyse the incident before bringing it to supervision because prior analysis can bias our exploration

NOTABLE INCIDENT EXAMPLE

Pat's Notable Incident

Background

I had to take an emergency phone call from an important client. Bruce is the head of one of the big businesses I consult to. He had to make an urgent decision that needed my input. Unfortunately, the call went on longer than I expected, so it made me 35 minutes late for my next appointment with a new counselling client, Dawn.

Incident

When I walk into the waiting room to greet Dawn she is sitting with her arms across her chest and looking at the floor. I notice that I feel uneasy. When I introduce myself Dawn jumps up and shakes hands rather stiffly. She smiles, but it's forced. I notice her eyes are puffy. Perhaps she's been crying?

I realise she's probably angry because she's been kept waiting. I assume the receptionist didn't pass on my apologies and my reason for keeping her waiting. I feel annoyed. I make a mental note to talk to the receptionist later. I also feel guilty that I kept Dawn waiting. I decide I'll make up for this bad start by being very professional and organised.

As we take our seats I apologise and then quickly get down to business. Dawn answers my questions very flatly. I realise she'll be hard to engage. I ask a question and she doesn't say anything. She is closed. Why? Should I apologise again for being late? But I've already apologised. There's no point in repeating it. It's frustrating. How can I get her to talk?

Suddenly there's a loud, sharp noise very close by. We are both startled. I look around and realise that a gust of wind has slammed the window shut. I settle quickly from the shock, but Dawn starts sobbing and holding herself tightly. I acknowledge her distress and sit quietly with her. She becomes easy to engage. She starts to tell me what's happening for her. She witnessed a car accident on the way here and only just managed to avoid being involved. I provide a safe space for her to debrief. Once she has settled we agree to make another appointment for next week.

Significance

I'm shocked that I couldn't engage with Dawn because I misinterpreted her distress as anger.

REFLECTIVE JOURNAL
HELIUM BALLOONS

Purpose: To reflect on what you've read, heard or experienced to help you to "get it"

HELIUM BALLOON METAPHOR

Imagine that there's nothing except hot air in your head from the level of your ears up. Information flows in one ear encased in a helium balloon. The balloon rolls around in the hot air and escapes out the other ear in just a few seconds. The only way to prevent it escaping is to tie it to your brain. To do this you need to attend fully to the information and process it in terms of what it means to you and how it could be useful.

If you simply notice it and think, "that's good", then all that you'll retain is "it was good". The actual content will be lost. Tie down what you want to keep by writing it in a helium balloon.

Tying it down is the first step, but helium balloons go flat within a few days. To retain the information it needs to be embedded in the brain and the only way to do that is to consolidate it by putting it into practice (E5).

How to use:
In training sessions – stop every hour or so (or after each module) and take a few minutes to "catch" some balloons. The learning is likely to be remembered even more if you then hear yourself tell it to someone else.

In supervision – stop now and then and either ask the two questions on the next page, or ask the practitioner to fill in one or more balloons. Discuss their choices to further "thicken" their understanding.

Follow up: Note the item "Action taken" at the bottom of the form. If the new learning isn't put into action it will be lost. It's worth coming back to the form at a later date and noting what action was taken and what more needs to be done to consolidate the learning.

Background: The helium balloon tool was developed by Daphne Hewson for use in supervision workshops. When the Psychology Board of Australia (PsyBA) introduced the requirement of Reflective Journals to record learnings from peer consultation, the form was adapted (see www.reflectivesupervision) to a format to meet their requirement. Note that the Board only accepts Reflective Journals that have the "Action Taken" section completed.

REFLECTIVE JOURNAL

What did you find most interesting or helpful?
What are the implications for your practice?

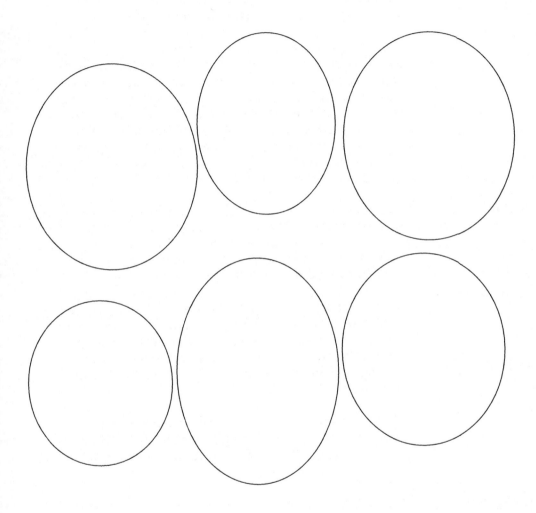

ACTION TAKEN

SUPERVISION TRIANGLE

Purpose:
The Supervision Triangle is a template of the areas that often need to be addressed in supervision.

Many supervision sessions seem to focus on the client and their problem (client-focused side of the triangle). If that's all that you consider, then supervision becomes case management (A2). The practitioner-focused side explores the practitioner's role and impact on the work, including reflexivity in the Self cell. The relationship-focused side explores the clients' relationships with the practitioner and their social system. It also shines a light on the supervisory relationship.

How to use:
We suggest you work around the template systematically, starting from the Client-focused cell – Assessment and Conceptualisation and heading up to the apex, down the other side and then across the bottom (left to right), finishing with the Supervisory relationship cell.

If information comes up that's relevant to another cell, you could put it aside until later. It can be tempting to skip a cell, but that's often the very cell that has the most interesting ideas. The questions on the two pages after the triangle are guides to the sorts of things to explore in each cell.

Gathering reflections in each cell is the Mindful Stance (noticing; E1). The next step is to analyse the material (Consideration Stance, E3). This can be done with a tool such as the *Pleased Platform*.

Background:
Developed by Daphne Hewson (2002)

Video:
A 50 minute supervision session demonstrating the use of the *Supervision Triangle* and *Pleased Platform* is available on youtube.com (youtu.be/4k4hsog8Ops)

Before you start:
Ensure you are in a safe reflective space

SUPERVISION TRIANGLE

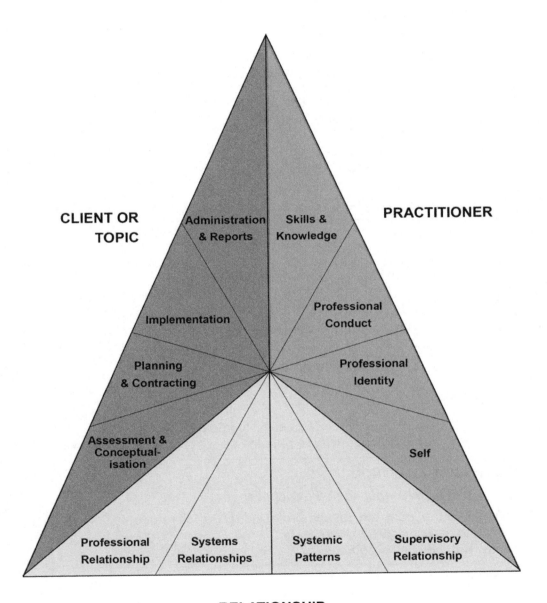

CLIENT OR TOPIC

PRACTITIONER

Administration & Reports

Skills & Knowledge

Professional Conduct

Implementation

Professional Identity

Planning & Contracting

Assessment & Conceptualisation

Self

Professional Relationship

Systems Relationships

Systemic Patterns

Supervisory Relationship

RELATIONSHIP

SUPERVISION TRIANGLE

CLIENT FOCUSED or TOPIC-FOCUSED CELLS

ASSESSMENT & CONCEPTUALISATION

If your only tool is a hammer, everything looks like a nail

- What is the topic/issue/presenting problem?
- What methods have you used (will you use) to assess the situation?
- Any other issues or problems?
- What are the strengths and "non-problems"?
- What is your conceptualisation (or diagnosis) of what is happening?
- Is there another way of looking at it?

PLANNING AND CONTRACTING

- What was (is) your plan?
- If (*client's name*) was here now, what would he/she say about the plan?

IMPLEMENTATION

- What's happened?
- Do you need to modify your conceptualisation or plan?

ADMINISTRATION & REPORTING

- What are the relevant admin, file and reporting issues?

PRACTITIONER-FOCUSED CELLS

SKILLS AND KNOWLEDGE

- What skills and knowledge are needed to implement the plan?
- Have you had the opportunity to gain the necessary skills and knowledge?

PROFESSIONAL CONDUCT

Every situation has legal and ethical challenges

- What are the legal, ethical and professional issues (e.g. duty of care) that need to be considered here?
- How are they being addressed?

PROFESSIONAL IDENTITY   *Personal social* power (Hewson, 2016)

- Do you believe you have the expertise needed to implement the plan?
- Do you believe you have the legitimate right to take this role?
- In what ways does this approach fit with your values and worldview?

SUPERVISION TRIANGLE

SELF

- What feelings have you been having about this client/your work?
- I noticed ……… What are the feelings behind that?
- What's your "stuff" in this? How is it impacting on this work?
- Who were you being when you did this work?
- How does who you are affect what you notice?
- How effectively are you making "use of self"?
- Who does (*client's name*) remind you of?
- In what ways is this work triggering you or impacting on you?

RELATIONSHIP-FOCUSED CELLS

PROFESSIONAL RELATIONSHIP

- Are you customers for each other?
- What needs to happen to strengthen your alliance?

SYSTEMS RELATIONSHIPS

- Who are the stakeholders in this work?
- Have they each been involved appropriately (boundaries)?
- Who/what is the person's "community"?
- What are their cultural needs?
- Who is influencing this situation?
- In what ways is their influence helpful and not so helpful?
- Who's missing from the story?

SYSTEMIC PATTERNS

- What parallel process is operating?
  (recreation of a behaviour/ emotion from another relationship)
- What about complementary patterns?
  (e.g. victim/rescuer, stupid/intelligent, disabled/able)
- Are you experiencing any contagion of behaviours/feelings?
- In what ways are these patterns helpful or unhelpful?

SUPERVISORY RELATIONSHIP

The supervisory alliance must be "good enough" to do the work at hand (B8)

- Do you feel safe enough for us to do this work together?
- What could I do to make it more helpful for you?
- What are we NOT talking about? Why?

VALUES

Purpose: To unearth and articulate your values.

Much of reflective practice concerns values, but people are often unable to identify their values or put them into words.

How to use: We use this tool early in reflective supervision and return to it frequently, especially when the practitioner is stuck. It usually generates images and a value that give them a new perspective on their stuckness.

Background: Adapted from Russ Harris's (2011) adaption of Kelly Wilson's (2005) "Sweet Spot" exercise; presented at Acceptance and Commitment Therapy (ACT) workshop.

References: Wilson (2005) is summarised in Wilson and Sandoz (2010)

VALUES

- Bring to mind a memory that conveys some of the richness of your working life (your own experience as a practitioner or observing someone else's work or reading an inspiring author)

  - Make it vivid (colour, smell, bodily sensations, etc.)
  - Notice all the feelings that arise (might include sadness)

- Share the memory as if it is happening in the present moment (use first person, present tense).

  While the person is sharing their memory the mindful listener does not speak. Give full attention to being with their story as though sitting with a sunset, not with a maths problem.

- When the person has finished sharing their memory, the listener asks:

  - What does this memory reveal about what matters to you?
  - What personal qualities were you showing?
  - How were you treating yourself, others, the world around you?
  - What does this tell you about what you stand for (what your values are)?
  - What does this suggest about the way you'd like to do things?
  - What name would you give to this value?

Adapted from Russ Harris's adaption of the "Sweet Spot" exercise (Wilson, 2005; Harris, 2011)
Sunset/maths problem imagery from Wilson and Sandoz (2010)

Purpose: To provide insights on difficulties that need to be tackled

The model is based on the theory that your weaknesses are not the opposite of your strengths but too much of them (e.g. determination becomes bullying or loyalty becomes collusion)

How to use: Go through the four components and explain what each means. Complete the table and then discuss "How can I meet the challenge of holding my core quality without it falling into being too much of a good or bad thing?"

Background: From Ofman (2001). The model of core qualities was originally devised for Human Resources managers to help them to give feedback in a more positive and helpful manner.

References: Ofman (2001), Carroll and Gilbert (2011)

CORE QUALITIES

CORE QUALITY ***Something done consistently well*** e.g., loyalty, determination, patience	**PITFALL** ***Too much of a good thing*** Loyalty becomes collusion Determination becomes bullying Patience becomes passivity

CORE QUALITY → **Too much** → PITFALL

Opposites

Opposites

ALLERGY ***What I can't stand in myself and others*** Loyalty can't stand betrayal Determination can't stand uncommitted Patience can't stand impatience	**CHALLENGE** ***How do I hold on to my core quality and not fall into my pit*** Loyalty needs objectivity Determination needs respect Patience needs assertiveness

CHALLENGE → **Too much** → ALLERGY

My Core Quality	My Pitfall	My Challenge	My Allergy
e.g. Loyalty	e.g. Collusion	e.g. Objectivity	e.g. Betrayal

How can I meet the challenge of holding my core quality
without falling into being too much of a good or bad thing?

From Ofman (2001) with permission from Scriptum Publishers

Purpose: To surface the practitioner's preferred actions, values and principles as a platform from which to reconsider other aspects of the work. This is an example of a "scaffolding" approach (James et al., 2008).

Practitioners often focus on problems and what went wrong. They take what they do well for granted and don't recognise their strengths. This tool shifts their focus from what they're displeased about to what they're pleased about.

How to use: This is Daf's favourite tool. It seems to be adaptable to so many situations. Here are some tips for using it.

- Keep bringing the practitioner back to the "pleased" question despite their frequent shifts back to problems. You can make a note of problems they raise, promise you'll get to them later, and then repeat the "pleased" question

- Keep asking the "pleased" question when they hit a blank. The blank just means they've run out of the safe or superficial ideas of their conscious mind. Wait patiently. You can use focusing methods (Scan your body, what do you notice, sit with that, what comes up for you now?), ask them to guess what else there might be, or ask them to externalise the gaze ("What would your elder be pleased about" or "What do you think I'm pleased about?"). Keep asking the "pleased" question at least three times after a blank. They'll start to unearth some interesting material!

- Thicken each response. You can write down their exact words and then ask for meaning, link them back to what they previously said, ask about how they managed to do what they did, ask how committed they are to an idea, etc.

- The "What would you like to do (to have done) differently?" question usually elicits from the practitioner all the suggestions you would have made and sometimes others that you hadn't thought of. By identifying them, the practitioner owns them and is more committed to them than if you suggest them.

- If you've asked "What else?" about 5 times and the practitioner hasn't named an issue that you think is important, raise it by "noticing" and then asking for their thoughts about it (e.g. I notice you seem to avoid eye contact with the client, but you use lots of good eye contact with me. I wonder why you chose to do it this way with the client?)

Background: Developed by Daphne Hewson

Before you start: Ensure you are in a safe reflective space

PP
PLEASED PLATFORM

1. IDENTIFY ISSUES/CHALLENGES

- Brief outline of relevant information (e.g. using notable incident or supervision triangle)
- What did you find most interesting or helpful in our conversation?
- Which aspects are you most interested in focusing on?

2. PLEASED PLATFORM

- What are you most pleased about?
  (or *Choose an esteemed person* – What would xx be pleased about in this work?)
- How did *you* do that?
- What else? (until list of 5+)
  (Don't stop when they hit a blank – the next "pleased" is likely to be the most significant one)

3. DO DIFFERENTLY?

- What would you like to do (to have done) differently?
- What else? (until list of 5+)
- Are any guidelines relevant here?

4. FEEDBACK

- I noticed that… (*positive or problematic behaviour*).
- In what ways is that helpful or not helpful for your clients?
- In what ways is that helpful or not helpful for you?
- What do you want to do about…?

5. CONSOLIDATION

- What have you found most helpful or interesting in our conversation?
- How will you refine your practice framework?
- What impact will this have on your actions?
- Why do you need to make this change?
- How do you plan to put it into practice?
- What are the restraints and how will you deal with them?
- What are you ready for now?

	SIS
	SLOGAN-INCIDENT-SLOGAN

Purpose: To surface and label some values, assumptions or principles (slogans) that underpin the practitioner's current actions and feelings and to explore some alternatives that might be preferred.

There are usually many themes in any notable incident or story. Noticing them and putting them into a slogan (short enough to print on a t-shirt) makes the assumptions vivid and easier to work with.

How to use: We use SIS often with the Self-Care Grid and also when we sense that there's an unclear theme in the practitioner's story. Practitioners sometimes take a while to get the idea of developing a slogan. You could make some very tentative suggestions to get them started. Once they find a slogan that fits, they get the idea and are able to use the tool much more easily thereafter.

The first slogan doesn't have to be good or bad, or helpful or unhelpful. It just has to be a saying that captures the theme/value/assumption/principle of their story. Whatever the slogan, ask for a recent incident that was contrary to it. You can be confident that whatever the slogan that's come up, it's got current relevance to the practitioner's work.

The second slogan, based on the recent incident, might be contrary to the first. The practitioner then reflects on both slogans and identifies which they prefer, and why. Sometimes the second slogan has equal valence to the first, and the discussion focuses on how to incorporate (or exclude) both from their practice (maybe front and back of the same t-shirt or two different t-shirts for different situations).

Background: Developed by Daphne Hewson and Judi Muller

Before you start: Ensure you are in a safe reflective space

SIS
SLOGAN-INCIDENT-SLOGAN

IDENTIFY ISSUE/CHALLENGE

- Brief outline of relevant information (e.g. using notable incident)

SLOGAN – IDENTIFY THE BASIC PRINCIPLE/ASSUMPTION/VALUE

- What do you notice in what you've told me?
- What theme/principle/value is implicit in what you've told me?
- Can you state that as a "slogan" short enough to put on a t-shirt? (*e.g. 'Be for others'*)
- Any other slogans?
- Are these slogans helpful or unhelpful for you? Why?

INCIDENT

- Could you tell me about a specific time when [contrary situation]

REFLECTION

- Tell me more about .... (keyword/concept/binary)
- How did you manage to do...?
- Why is it important?
- What does ... (*word or image*) mean to you?
- Are any guidelines relevant here?

SLOGAN – IDENTIFY PREFERRED PRINCIPLE/ASSUMPTION/VALUE

- What's most interesting in what we've been talking about?
- What theme/principle/value is implicit in that?
- Can you state that as a t-shirt "slogan"?
- How does that fit with... (previous slogan)?
- "Thicken" the concept. e.g.:
  Who would be least surprised that you would choose this slogan?
  What do they know about you to predict you'd choose it?
  How does having this slogan affect your view of yourself?"

CONSOLIDATION

- What have you found most helpful or interesting in our conversation?
- How will you refine your practice framework?
- What impact will this have on your actions?
- Why do you need to make this change?
- How do you plan to put it into practice?
- What are the restraints and how will you deal with them?
- What are you ready for now?

WANAW
Well and Not as Well

Purpose:
To identify preferred goals and actions. This tool is similar to SIS, except that SIS focuses on underlying assumptions (slogans), while WANAW focuses on behaviours.

When practitioners express concern about a piece of work, their concern usually arises because it didn't go as well as previous work.

WANAW draws on their expertise in other situations as the marker for considering the problematic situation.

How to use:
Firstly, explore the problematic situation.

Write down what happened and didn't happen, actions, thoughts, emotions, assumptions, etc.

Then choose a recent, similar situation that "went well" (you can be sure that there is one, it just might take a few minutes for the practitioner to think of it).

Explore it in similar detail. Write it down.

Then compare the two lists.

Background:
Developed by Daphne Hewson

Before you start: Ensure you are in a safe reflective space

WANAW
Well and Not as Well

IDENTIFY THE CHALLENGE

- Identify an event that didn't go well
- What were you trying to achieve?
- How did you approach it? How did you do it? (list all of these)

WHAT WENT WELL

- Think of a time recently when ..... went well. (e.g. if lack of engagement is the issue, "think of a time recently when you engaged well with a client")
- What were you trying to achieve?
- What did you do? How did you do it? (Continue questions until you've listed very specific details on approach and methods)

FEEDBACK

- I noticed that .... (*positive or problematic behaviour*).
- In what ways was that helpful or not helpful?
- Is there anything else we could add to these two lists?
- Are any guidelines or research evidence relevant here?

COMPARISONS

- Let's compare the two lists. These are your goals, approaches and methods when it went well and when it didn't go as well. What do you notice?
- What held you back from putting your preferred approach and values into practice?
- What are the principles you want to take from this?

CONSOLIDATION

- What have you found most helpful or interesting in our conversation?
- How will you refine your practice framework?
- What impact will this have on your actions?
- Why do you need to make this change?
- How do you plan to put it into practice?
- What are the restraints and how will you deal with them?
- What are you ready for now?

Purpose: To provide a brief, but broad, reflection of an experience.

Why Ask Why? Professionals are often surprised to see the question "Why". They were taught not to ask it in their basic training. We agree that if a client says, "I'm depressed", then asking Why? is not helpful. But it can be a helpful question when the person has expressed a strong belief. For example, in Narrative therapy, Michael White elicited the person's preferred values or way of being and then thickened their appreciation of them by asking Why?

The potential problem with Why? is that it can lead to confabulation (Wilson, 2002; see discussion in Chapter C1). People don't know that their nonconscious mind made a decision, so they give a rational explanation from their conscious mind. But their "other mind" probably used other, much more complex reasons. Their confabulated answer can shape their future decision making in the short term.

When we learnt about the confabulation problem we baulked at using AARY. But unpacking assumptions is fundamental to reflective supervision, so in a sense, most of our questions are forms of Why? The research shows that the impact of the confabulation is short-lived because the nonconscious mind takes control again as soon as the conscious mind stops paying attention to the subject. Also, in supervision we can unpack the proffered reasons and expand on them. We can use the conscious minds ideas as a helpful starting point for discussion without believing that it has given a full and accurate account.

It's helpful if the practitioner is aware of this issue so they don't experience further probing as a mistrust of their honesty. Their conscious mind can be very honest, but very wrong!

How to use: Ask "Why?" as a supportive/challenge question, not as a blaming/shaming put-down. Then explore more deeply. Ensure the practitioner understands that the probing is not a mistrust of their honesty, but an attempt to unearth the assumptions that are outside of their consciousness.

Background: Adapted from AAR as used by American Military debriefing of troops in Kuwait and Iraq. The additions are the question about feelings (thanks Bronwyn Partridge) and the "Why" questions

References: Garvin (2000; cited by Carroll, 2010), Schooler & Engstler-Schooler (1990), White (Evaluate and justify questions; 2005), Wilson and Schooler (1991), Wilson et al. (1989), Wilson (2002)

Before you start: Ensure you are in a safe reflective space

AARY
After Action Review. Why?

- What did you set out to do?
  Why?

- How did you go about it?
  Why?

- Does this fit with relevant guidelines?
  How? Or why not?

- What feelings have you experienced?
  Why?

- What was the outcome?
  Why?

- What went well?
  Why?

- What didn't go so well?
  Why?

- What have you learned?
  Why is it important to learn this?

- What will you do differently next time?
  Why?

WACA
What-Analysis-Conceptualisation-Action

Purpose: To provide a broad, but brief reflection on an experience with more detail than AARY.

The letters WACA are a reminder of the phases of Kolb's experiential learning spiral (A3).

How to use: The questions are guides to the areas to address in a brief reflective session. Choose those that fit the context allowing enough time to consolidate the new learning (Conceptualisation and Action Plan)

Background: Adapted from Kolb (1984) and Johns (2009) model of structured reflection.

Before you start: Ensure you are in a safe reflective space

WACA
What-Analysis-Conceptualisation-Action

WHAT HAPPENED?

- Describe a concrete experience
- What were you trying to achieve?
- What were you thinking?
- What were you feeling?
- What was the other person thinking and feeling?
- What was good and not so good about the experience?
- What are the main issues?

ANALYSIS

- Why did you do what you did?
- Are any guidelines relevant here? What were your assumptions?
- How did these assumptions influence your thinking and behaviour?
- What external factors influenced your thinking and behaviour?
- How do your actions fit with your beliefs?
- What choices did you have?
- What could you have done differently?
- What would be the consequences of making a different choice?

CONCEPTUALISATION

- What have you found most helpful or interesting in our conversation?
- What are the principles you want to take from this?
- How will you refine your practice framework?
- What impact will this have on your actions?
- Why do you need to make this change?

ACTION PLAN

- How do you plan to put your new learning into practice?
- What support do you need?
- What are the restraints and how will you deal with them?
- What are you ready for now?

ROAM
Reflecting On A Moment

Purpose: To reflect on behaviour and internal experiences during a moment of the event.

When practitioners overview their work they miss the moment-by-moment details. Kagan's (1980) Interpersonal Process Recall approach is used in supervision when reviewing a recording of a session. The tape is paused when something catches the attention of either the supervisor or practitioner and they reflect on the details of the moment (actions, thoughts, feelings, expectations, assumptions, etc.). This tool adapts the same process to reflecting on moments in the notable incident. It involves imagining being in-the-moment to re-experience details of the moment to enrich the reflective process.

How to use: ROAM is intended as a brief tool to embed within the reflective process. It's particularly useful when you notice decision points. Asking the practitioner to relive the moment is likely to unearth assumptions that wouldn't be noticed if they simply talked "about" the event from a distance.

When using ROAM, stay with the spirit of the tool – to focus in on the moment-by-moment experience – and choose questions that fit the momentary context.

Background: Adapted from Bernstein and Lecomte (1979), Neufeldt (1999), Bennett-Levy et al. (2009). Based on Kagan's (1980) Interpersonal Process Recall

Before you start: Ensure you are in a safe reflective space

ROAM
Reflecting On A Moment

FOCUS ON THE MOMENT
- Focus on a moment during the session/experience as though it's happening now
- What do you notice?

REFLECTIONS

BEHAVIOUR
- What was your intention?
- How did you choose from among the possible actions?
- What was the result of what you did? Is this helpful? Or unhelpful?

EMOTIONS
- What were you feeling? What are you feeling now?
- How do you understand those feelings?
- What was the emotional flavour of the interaction?
- Is that similar or different from the usual interactions?
- Do you think the other person was aware of your feelings?
- What do you think they were feeling?

COGNITIONS
- What were you thinking?
- What images or memories were flashing through your mind?
- What were you expecting to happen?
- What do you think the other person was thinking?
- What were they expecting to happen?
- What message do you think they were trying to give you?
- What past experiences affected your understanding?
- What theories did you use to understand what was going on?
- How do you understand what was happening between you?

ANALYSIS AND CONSOLIDATION
- What were the assumptions at the time?
- Are any guidelines or research findings relevant here?
- How would you now evaluate the experience?
- How does this experience affect your professional sense of self?
- What have you found most helpful or interesting in our conversation?
- How will you refine your practice framework?
- What impact will this have on your actions?
- Why do you need to make this change?
- How do you plan to put it into practice?
- What are the restraints and how will you deal with them?
- What are you ready for now?

LENSES

Purpose: To gain a 360-degree perspective by viewing an experience through a range of different reflective lenses. Each lens focuses on the experience from a different perspective.

How to use: Ensure safe reflective space.
Read the description of each lens and then discuss what you notice about the presenting issue (The Experience in the diagram overleaf) when you look at it through each lens. Consolidate the learning by articulating the concepts and planning how to implement them.
A good question for supervisors: *"What is the appropriate lens to use at this moment that best connects the practitioner to where they are and challenges them to access the next stage of their learning?"*

Background: Developed by Michael Carroll (2009, 2010). The lenses were originally published as six "levels". We have changed the term "levels" to "lens" to indicate that they are different ways of looking, not necessarily deeper or better levels. Originally one of the "levels" was zero-reflection (what was called ME: External Reflection). We have not included this non-reflective stance as a reflective lens. When someone is in zero-reflection space, the aim is to use questions from the other lens to support them to shift to a reflective stance and view the situation through other lenses.

LENS 1: THEM reflection

The perspective of the other person or people involved in the event

"I can understand why the person does this, although that does not excuse it"

The self becomes an observer of others and events.
While empathy is needed to acknowledge other perspectives and stances, it tends to be intellectual empathy rather than emotional empathy.
There is some compassion in the meaning making (but to a limited degree)

LENS 2: US: Relational reflection

The relationship(s) between the practitioner and each of the others

"Now I see that it's about you and me and how we are getting on together"

Awareness that issues, events, problems and experiences can be relational and not just belong to one person.
We co-create many issues in our lives.
We take up a position of shared responsibility.

LENS 3: SYSTEMS: Systemic reflection

a) **Their Systems**: All the relevant people and systems involved with them in some way such as referral person, family, friends, community, their organisation, professional association and social systems (e.g. health, education, legal, welfare)

b) **My Systems**: All the relevant people and systems involved with me in some way such as colleagues, manager, referral networks, my organisation and professional association, legal and ethical frameworks, family, friends and community

"How do our contexts and connections influence this situation?"

Look at systems and various subsystems that affect what's happening.
Use the helicopter metaphor to make sense of it from bigger viewpoints.
Review the bigger picture.
Explore how "context gives meaning" in this situation
Extend to shared resources and history that shape our choices and values – can extend into ancestry, heritage, community, culture and ecosystem.

LENS 4: ME: Internal Reflection.

The practitioner's part in this in terms of skills and knowledge, psychological context (such as mood), values and worldview

"Gosh, it's actually about me!"

Explore how the self plays a part in the situation
Awareness of self and own meaning-making perspectives.
Start to articulate own patterns and themes that contribute to the way the practitioner engages in life and relationships and this experience.

LENS 5: MEANING: Transcendent reflection

The perspective of religious, spiritual or philosophical positions

"From within my philosophy of life, how can I make sense of this event?"

Moving 'beyond" to what gives meaning to life, people and behaviour.
Transcending any particular relationship, person or situation.
Can be a religious or spiritual stance (e.g., Buddhist, Jewish, Christian, Muslim, Hindu, humanistic values etc.).
Gets in touch with bigger values that supersede particular ones (Rumi: "In the field beyond right and wrong, I will meet you there")

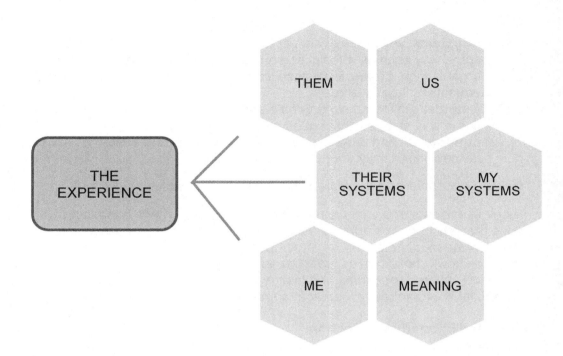

"THEM" LENS (THE OTHER or OTHERS)

- Who are the other people in this experience?
- How might they see it?
- How might they feel about it?
- What was most helpful in what they did or said?
- What difference does it make to understand it from their viewpoint?

"US" LENS (RELATIONSHIPS)

- What was happening in the relationship between you and them?
- What is it in your relationship with..... that has resulted in this outcome?
- Can you describe the relationship "dance" you have created with.....?
- What changes in the relationship might be helpful?
- What might need to change between you for you to have a better relationship?

"SYSTEMS" LENS   a) THEIR SYSTEMS   b) MY SYSTEMS

- Bateson said, "the context gives meaning". How might this apply here?

Their systems
- Who is involved with them? What systems are involved?
- In what way do these people/systems influence what happened?
- What was most helpful in what each of these people/systems did?
- How might their organisation and colleagues view it?
- How might these people/systems be more helpful?

My systems
- Who in your network is involved with this? Which of your systems is involved?
- In what way do these people/systems influence what happened?
- What might these people/system notice about this situation?
- What standards/guidelines/ethics/legal issues are relevant?
- What does the best practice literature tell you about it?

"ME (INTERNAL)" LENS

- Can you describe the role you played in this?
- What personal "stuff" did you bring to it (mood, stress levels, triggers, projections etc.)?
- How did your culture and background impact on you?
- What did you actually do, rather than what was your intention?
- What changes in you would make a difference here? (e.g., knowledge, skills, values)

"MEANING" LENS

- What values could you access to help you deal with this? (e.g., compassion, forgiveness, letting go, moving towards, accepting)
- What values could you adopt that would enable you to reflect in wider ways? (e.g., diversity, cooperation, autonomy)
- From your philosophy of life, how can you make sense of this?
- What really matters here?

CONSOLIDATION

- What has been most helpful in our conversation?
- What will you now highlight or change in your practice framework?
- What impact will our dialogue have on future actions?

Purpose: To unpack the practitioner's unsettling emotional responses. It's often possible to explore the practitioner's emotions with simple focusing methods, but sometimes more direct questions are needed.

For example, May expressed concerns about a situation that was developing in her workplace.

Supervisor:	Just sit with your concerns for a moment. What do you notice?
May:	A vague feeling through my body
Supervisor:	Can you give the feeling a name?
May:	Uncomfortable
Supervisor:	What colour is it?
May:	Blue.
Supervisor:	What does that blue mean to you?
May:	Unknown. Out of my element.
Supervisor:	Is the feeling directed towards a particular person or issue?
May:	Maybe a bit about some of the other people involved. Maybe a bit about the situation itself. But no clear focus.

The supervisor then introduced the EMAP and asked questions about each of the nine possible sources of emotional reactions. As a rough guide, the sources are categorised as Professional (work stuff), Personal (own stuff that's impacting on work) or Personal-Professional (impact of work stuff on self). Ignore these categories if they don't fit with your theoretical stance.

May recognised that:

- she was confused about her professional role
- she was experiencing a conflict between her values and the approach her manager wanted her to take
- she had become triangulated in a difficult relationship between two colleagues
- she was more sensitive to tension than usual because of a current health problem.

Before starting: Ensure you are in a safe reflective space

Background: Developed by Daphne Hewson and Marilyn Hadfield

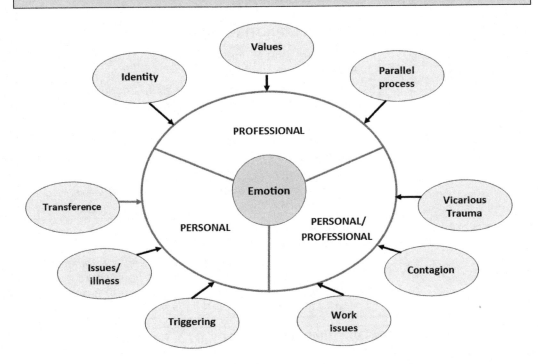

- Let's look at the different places the feeling could be coming from - work stuff, your stuff or the impact of work stuff on you

PROFESSIONAL (WORK STUFF)	
Identity	Expertise, role, sense of your legitimate rights and responsibilities • *What is your role in relation to this person/issue?* • *Do you feel confident you can fulfil your role?* • *Is there any tension or ambiguity around your role?*
Values/ethics	Your values and worldview, moral and ethical positioning • *In what ways does this situation fit with your values and worldview?* • *In what ways does it not fit?*
Parallel process	Parallel process – recreation of a behaviour/emotion from one relationship in another • *Who else is having this feeling?* • *In what ways is this parallel process helpful/unhelpful?*

PERSONAL (OWN STUFF THAT'S IMPACTING ON WORK)	
Personal issues/ stress/illness	Current life stress; unresolved personal issues, physical and mental health issues. • *How might any personal stress be impacting on this?* • *If this feeling belong somewhere else in your life?* • *What health issues might be impacting on this?*
Personal triggering	Triggering of own trauma/cultural material in response to characteristics of the situation • *Are any aspects of this personally triggering for you?* • *What were your family messages about the issues in this situation?*
Transference	Redirection of feeling from a significant person in the past to a current relationship • *Who are you most reminded of when you think about this person or about this person's behaviours?* • *In what ways are you responding as if to a person in your life rather than to what's happening here?*

PERSONAL-PROFESSIONAL (IMPACT OF WORK STUFF ON SELF)	
Vicarious trauma and Compassion fatigue	Trauma from being exposed to traumatic material; can lead to sensitisation (move threshold down) – become more aware and reactive to trauma material Compassion fatigue - exhaustion from long-term empathy with gradual lessening of compassion; can lead to desensitisation (move the threshold up) – less sensitivity to noticing or reacting to trauma material • *Did you see or hear any material that could be upsetting or traumatising?* • *Are you taking the traumatic feelings home with you?* • *Have you noticed any changes in your sensitivity to traumatic material?*
Contagion (emotional resonance)	Contagion (mirroring) "Catching" the other person's emotions from deep empathy or mirroring body position. (e.g. feeling down when working with depression) • *Have you been "catching" the emotions of others?*
Work stress/issues	Work overload; workplace conflict • *In what ways is your workload impacting on you?* • *Are there any workplace conflicts or issues that are impacting on you?*

REFLECTION

- Which of these processes do you think might be important here?
- If you saw your emotions as messengers, what do you think they might be communicating to you?
- How are these feelings useful for you?
- What impact are your emotions having on... (client, colleagues, family, others)?
- What stands out as most interesting or helpful in what we've been discussing?
- Why is it important to you?
- What methods do you have to manage/cope/respond to the emotions?
- In what ways are these methods helpful and unhelpful for you? (... to your client, colleagues, family, others?)
- What are your concerns now?
- Are any standards/guidelines relevant here?
- Is there an ethical challenge here? (e.g. duty of care)
- Whose responsibility is it to address this challenge?
- What do these reflections tell you about how power is operating in this situation?
- What do these reflections tell you about your socio-politico-cultural positioning?
- What do these reflections tell you about your values?
- What do they tell you about your professional identity and role?
- What do you notice overall about how your personal stuff is impacting on your work? (Do you think it would be helpful to seek some therapy?)
- What do you notice overall about how your work is impacting on you? (Do you need to make some changes in your work to protect yourself and your family?)

CONSOLIDATION

- What has been most interesting or helpful in this conversation?
- How will you refine your practice framework?
- What impact will this have on your actions?
- What do you need to do about all this?
- Why do you need to make these changes?
- How do you plan to put it into practice?
- What are the restraints and how will you address them?
- What are you ready for now?

UMM
Unpacking Multiple Meanings

Purpose: To seek rich, thick, deep, multiple meanings by using a range of different lenses and to unpack the assumptions underpinning these meanings

This tool helps you to learn to shift from reflection to critical reflection (C4). Many of the other tools include critical reflection questions, but they don't intentionally develop the critical stance.

The section on Alternatives/Preferred Stories borrows from White's narrative therapy. It identifies and builds preferred beliefs and values as a basis for reconstructing problematic assumptions.

How to use: Ensure the practitioner is aware that you are intentionally exploring their deeper assumptions and that they might find themselves on "the edge of meaning" (Berger, 2004). This tool is not a script. The questions are suggestions to unpack meaning and explore power practices.

Background: Developed by Daphne Hewson, Janet Conti and Adriana Glusman, adapting ideas and questions from Brookfield (1988), Fook and Gardner (2007), White (2007)

Before you start: Ensure you are in a safe reflective space

UMM
Unpacking Multiple Meanings

THE INCIDENT

- *Brief* description of the event (e.g. notable incident)
- Why is it significant for you?
- What is the **reflective focus** for this conversation?

UNPACKING MEANINGS

- What words have you used?
- What does … (*keywords or images*) mean to you?
- What does that word/image tell you about your beliefs?
- Are there any patterns?
- What binaries do you notice? (e.g. if x is important, who is unimportant?)
- What is missing in your story?
- Are there any contradictions in your story? (e.g. apparently opposing values)
- What other ways could the story be told (e.g. from another perspective)?
- What beliefs/values/commitments are behind your actions?
- In what ways are these ideas/beliefs helpful or unhelpful?

REFLEXIVITY

- How did what you were looking for influence what you found?
- How did your language construct what you saw?
- Who were you being when you were doing this work?
- What were you valuing?
- How has who you are affected what you noticed?
- What emotions and mood were you experiencing?
- How were they affecting what you noticed/did?
- What would have been different if someone else had been in your place?
- How did you influence the situation? (by what you did, by your presence, by your socio-politico-cultural position, by your perceptions, by other person's perceptions of you)

POWER

- In what ways was power operating in this situation?
- What do you see as your role (responsibility) in this situation?
- What do your actions imply about your beliefs about power?
- How is power being used in the relationship (by each party)?
- How are you each empowered and disempowered in this relationship?
- What are you resisting? What are they resisting?
- Are you valuing or demonising resistance?
- Whose interests seem to be served by your practices?
- What will happen to your self-image if you see yourself as having failed in respect to your good intentions?

"THE GAZE"

- What is a good...? (e.g. clinician, worker, manager, professional)
- Where did you learn that idea? Who from? What is their belief?

- Who was looking over your shoulder when you were in this situation?
- What were they telling you?
- What "should" you do?
- Who says you should do this? Who else?
- Why do they believe you should do it?
- In what ways is this belief helpful or unhelpful to you? Why?
- How does that belief fit with your values?

- Who were you comparing yourself with?
- How does this person's ... (behaviour/standards/values) fit with your values?

- What are the dominant discourses operating here?
- Where do you position yourself in terms of the various discourse communities?

ASSUMPTIONS

- What assumptions have you unearthed?
- What are the connections between them?
- Can you identify a fundamental belief or value that underpins them?
- What name/label would you give it?
- How does it affect your view of yourself?
- In what ways is this helpful or unhelpful? Why?

ALTERNATIVES/PREFERRED STORIES

- What image do you have ... of the ideal situation?
- How did you come to have this image?
- What ideas/hopes inform this image?

- What are alternative perspectives or roles could you take?
- Are there times when you've done this?
- How did it go?
- What do you value about those times?
- What do those times say about what matters to you?
- How does knowing this affect your view of yourself?

CONSOLIDATION

- What have you found most interesting or helpful in our conversation?
- How will you refine your practice framework?
- Can you give it a name (label/slogan)?
- What will you do differently?
- Who do you want to have looking over your shoulder (being on your team)?
- What difference will this make to your practice?
- Why do you need to make this change?
- How do you plan to put it into practice?
- What are the restraints and how will you deal with them?
- What are you ready for now?

REFERENCES

American Psychological Association (2010) *Self-care for psychologists.* www.apapracticecentral.org/update/2010/08-31/survey.aspx

Bennett-Levy, J. Thwaites, R., Chaddock, A. and Davis, M. (2009) Reflective practice in cognitive behavioural therapy. Ch 7 in J. Stedmon & R. Dallos (eds.) *Reflective Practice in Psychotherapy and Counselling.* McGraw Hill.

Bennett-Levy, J., Thwaites, R. Haarhoff, B. and Perry, H. (2015) *Experiencing CBT from the inside out. A self-practice/self-reflection workbook.* Guilford.

Berger, J.G. (2004) Dancing on the threshold of meaning: recognizing and understanding the growing edge. *Journal of Transformative Education*, 2, 336-351.

Bernstein, B & Lecomte, C. (1979) Self-critique technique training in a competency-based practicum. *Counselor Education and Supervision*, 19, 69-76.

Brookfield, S. (1988) Developing critically reflective practitioners. In S. Brookfield (ed.) *Training Educators of Adults.* Routledge.

Carroll, M. (2009) From mindless to mindful practice: on learning reflection in supervision. *Psychotherapy in Australia,* 15, 4, 38-49.

Carroll, M. (2010) Levels of reflection. *Psychotherapy in Australia,* 16, 2, 24-31.

Carroll, M. and Gilbert, M. (2005) *On being a supervisee.* Vukani Pubs; PsychOz. (2nd Ed. 2011).

CRCP Center for Reflective Community Practice (2011) *Critical Moments Reflection.* Massachusetts Institute of Technology. www.kstoolkit.org

Duncan, B., Miller, S., Sparks, J., Claud, D., Reynolds, L. Brown, J. & Johnson, L. (2003) The session rating scale. *Journal of Brief Therapy*, 3, 3-12.

Duncan, B. Miller, S., Wampold, B & Hubble, M. (Eds.) (2009) *The heart and soul of change: delivering "what works".* APA Press.

Fook, J. and Gardner, F. (2007) *Practising critical reflection: A resource handbook.* Open University Press.

Green, D. and Latchford, G. (2012) *Maximising the benefits of psychotherapy. A practice-based evidence approach.* Wiley-Blackwell.

James, I., Milne, D. and Morse, R. (2008) Microskills of clinical supervision: scaffolding skills. *Journal of Cognitive Psychotherapy*, 22, 29-36.

Johns, C. (2009) *Guided reflection: Advancing practice.* Wiley.

Harris, R. (2011)   ACT workshop notes. www.actmindfully.com.au

Hewson, D. (2002) A supervision triangle. In M. McMahon & W. Patton, (eds.) *Supervision in the helping professional.* Pearson Education.

Hewson, D. (2016) *Social power in supervision.* www.reflectivesupervision.com

Inskipp, F. & Proctor, B. (1993) *The art, craft and tasks of counselling supervision. Part 1. Making the most of supervision.* Cascade.

Kagan, N. (1980) Influencing human interaction – eighteen years with IPR. In A.K. Hess (Ed.), *Psychotherapy supervision.* 262-283. Wiley.

Kegan, R. and Lahey, L. (2009) *Immunity to change.* Harvard Business Press.

Kline, N. (1999) *Time to think. Listening to ignite the human mind.* Ward Lock.

Kline, N. (2009) *More time to think.* Fisher King Pub.

Kolb, D. (1984) *Experiential learning.* Prentice Hall.

Lahad, M. (2000) *Creative Supervision: the use of expressive arts methods in supervision and self-Supervision.* Jessica Kingsley.

Lambert, M. & Shimokawa, K. (2011) Collecting client feedback. Ch 10 in J.C.Norcross (Ed.), *Psychotherapy relationships that work.* 2nd Ed. Oxford University Press.

Loehr, J. and Schwartz, T. (2003) *On form.* Nicholas Brealey Pub.

Maeschalck, C., Bargmann, S., Miller, S.D. and Bertolino, B. (2012) *Feedback-Informed Supervision.* ICCE Manual 3. Int. Center for Clinical Excellence.

Miller, S.D. (2011) *Psychometrics of ORS and SRS.* wwwslideshare.net/

Minuchin, S. and Fishman, H. (1981) *Family therapy techniques.* Harvard Uni.

Neufeldt, S.A. (1999) Training in reflective processes (pp 92-105). In E. Holloway and M. Carroll (eds.). *Training Counselling Supervisors.* Sage.

Ofman, D. (2001) *Core qualities: a gateway to human resources.* Scriptum Publishers.

Schooler, J. and Engstler-Schooler, T. (1990) Verbal overshadowing: some things are better left unsaid. *Cognitive Psychology, 22* 36-71.

Schuck, C. and Wood, J. (2011) *Inspiring creative supervision.* Jessica Kingsley.

scottmiller.com (up-to-date information on Feedback)

Wainwright, N. (2010) *The development of the Leeds Alliance in Supervision Scale (LASS). A brief sessional measure of the supervisory alliance.* Doctoral thesis. University of Leeds. (LASS reproduced in Green & Latchford, 2012).

White, M. (2005) www.dulwichcentre.com.au/michael-white-workshopnotes.pdf

White, M. (2007) *Maps of narrative practice.* Norton.

Wilson, K.G. & Sandoz, E. K. (2010) Mindfulness, values, and the therapeutic relationship in ACT. In S. Hick & T. Bein (Eds.) *Mindfulness and the therapeutic relationship.* Guilford.

Wilson, T. (2002) *Strangers to ourselves.* Harvard University Press

Wilson, T. and Schooler, J. (1991) Thinking too much. *Journal of Personality and Social Psychology, 60,* 2, 181-192.

Wilson, T., Dunn, D., Kraft, D., & Lisle, D. (1989). The disruptive effects of explaining why we feel the way we do. In L. Berkowitz (Ed.), *Advances in experimental social psychology, 19,* (123-205). Academic Press.

MINI-TOOLS FOR NOTICING (from E2)

Positives

- What are you most pleased about?
- What would [your elder] be pleased about in this?

Perspectives

- What do you notice in this?
- What do you think I notice in this?
- What would ..... notice in that?

Nancy Kline's Thinking Questions ™

- What are your thoughts on this?
- What more do you think or feel or want to say?
- What more?

Language

- What does ..... mean?
- What name would you give that?
- You've used the metaphor (image) of .... What does .... mean to you?

Absent but expected

- What's missing from this account?
- When was the first critical moment?
- What are we not talking about?
- Is there anything you deliberately don't bring to supervision? Why?

Relive the moment

- What were you feeling at that moment? And what were they feeling?
- What were you thinking at that moment? And what were they thinking?
- What were you expecting at that moment? And what were they expecting?

MINI-TOOLS FOR NOTICING (from E2)

Inner experience

- You seem to be holding yourself tightly as you talk. What does the tightness mean?
- Where do you feel that in your body? Stay with that feeling.
- What do you notice?
- Can you name that feeling?
- Are you feeling embarrassed or ashamed about anything?

Disrupt autopilot

- Which parts of this are part of your routine?
- I notice that you …… Is that the usual way you do it?

Relationships

- Is your relationship with (client) "good enough" for what you're trying to do together?
- What is he/she a customer for?
- Are you customers for each other?
- Are there any ways you're feeling disconnected from me?
- Are you feeling safe enough?

Tools and Conceptualisation

- What methods have you used to assess the situation?
- What is your conceptualisation (or diagnosis) of what's happening?
- How did the tools you used shape what you know about this situation/client?

Frame

- How have you framed the problem?
- What name would you give this frame?

MINI-TOOLS FOR NOTICING (from E2)
(continued)

Espoused Theory and Theories-in-use

- What were you trying to achieve?
- What was your plan (method) for meeting your goal?
- How can we summarise that goal and plan?
- What did you actually do (and not do)?
- What theories-in-use are implicit in that?

Self and Role

- How does who you are impact on what's happening here?
- Who were you being when you did this work?
- How are you making "use of self" in this work?
- Who is responsible for what?
- How do your own psychological processes impact on what's happening here?
- Who does ..... remind you of?
- Are you being triggered by this work?

Systemic Patterns

- How might parallel process be operating here?
- What about complementary roles?

Competency

- Have you had the opportunity to gain the skills and knowledge necessary to .....?

Professional conduct

- What are the legal, ethical and professional challenges in this situation?
- What's your duty of care?

D. Hewson and M. Carroll *Reflective Supervision Toolkit*

MINI-TOOLS FOR CONSIDERATION (from E4)

Marking

- What did you find most interesting or helpful?

Instinct

- What does your gut instinct tell you about this?

Thicken the account

- How did you do that?
- And what else?

Language and metaphors

- You used the word ..... What would be different if we used the word .... instead?
- What name (metaphor) could we use for that?
- The image (metaphor) that comes to mind for me is ..... What are your thoughts on that?

The "helpful" question

- In what ways is it helpful and not so helpful?

Absent but implicit

- What values are implicit in .....?
- You described xxx as ..... What does this imply about .....?

Visual depiction

- Can you draw a picture to visually depict this [theory] [relationship]?
- Can you map these concepts?
- The image I get is this [draw picture or map]. Does that capture the idea?

MINI-TOOLS FOR CONSIDERATION (from E4)
(continued)

Shift a characteristic

- What would you have done differently if the person was xxx?
- What does this tell you about your assumptions about xxx?

Concepts

- What concepts can we draw upon to understand this?

Theories-in-use

- What did you actually say and do (and not say and not do)?
- What assumptions and values are suggested by your actions?
- I noticed ..... What does that imply about your assumptions?
- I noticed ..... I wonder if that means you are assuming ..... ?

Kegan and Lahey's Competing Commitments

- What are you afraid will happen if your commitment is met?

Frames

- You've framed the problem as... How might someone else frame it?
- What assumptions led to you framing it in that way?

Recurring themes

- I remember that in the past we also discussed ... when we talked about other clients. Perhaps there's a theme here?
- Have you noticed this concern in your work with other clients?
- Does this situation remind you of one in your past?
- What's the common assumption in these experiences?

Values and vision

- How does this work fit with your values and vision?
- Is there anything about this work that bothers you?
- How could you modify your goals or methods so they fit better with your values?

D. Hewson and M. Carroll *Reflective Supervision Toolkit*

MINI-TOOLS FOR CONSIDERATION (from E4)
(continued)

Systemic Influences

- Who are the stakeholders in this and what impact are they having?
- How do their needs and rules fit with your ideas?

The Gaze

- Whose gaze is shaping how you approach this?
- Where did you learn the idea that you are supposed to think this?
- What would your grandparents say about this?
- Who do you want on your team?
- What would they say?

Psychological Processes

- How would someone whose [transference, countertransference, personal issue] wasn't being triggered respond in this situation?
- We've noticed that the roles of [weak/strong; victim/rescuer; parent/child] have developed in your relationship.
- What assumptions are holding you in your role?

Processing ruptures

- What's happening between us?
- What is this triggering for you?
- What can I do to make this safer for you?

Addressing shame and other troubles

- What needs to happen for you to be able to work with this vulnerability?

Brainstorming

- What other approaches might have been possible?
- Let's try to think of as many different ways of interpreting this as possible

MINI-TOOLS FOR CONSIDERATION (from E4)
(continued)

Cultural practices

- Whose notions of what's normal are being applied here?
- Who benefits from this approach?
- And who is disadvantaged?
- How does this approach support current social attitudes and arrangements?

CRCP's Critical moments

- Think back before this incident (hours, days, weeks). What are the moments, either positive or negative, that were critical shifts in how this experience unfolded?
- How much agency did you feel you had at each of these critical moments?
- I wonder why you chose to ....?

Berger's "the edge"

- Can you sit with that feeling for a moment? What do you notice?
- What values or assumptions are being shaken?
- What do you need to feel safe enough to explore this assumption?
- Are you ready to explore that assumption a bit more today?

Nancy Kline's Incisive Question ™

- What are you assuming that is most limiting your thinking here?
- Is that assumption true?
- What is a liberating true alternative to the limiting assumption?
- If you knew [insert the true alternative], what would you think or feel or do?

Challenge assumptions

- What's the evidence to support this belief?
- What would you prefer to believe?

D. Hewson and M. Carroll *Reflective Supervision Toolkit*

MINI-TOOLS FOR CONSIDERATION (from E4)
(continued)

Elicit preferred action

- What would you like to have done differently?
- If I were to suggest what you could do, what do you think I'd suggest?

Summarising Mindful-Consideration Stances

- What assumptions were unearthed for you and what main themes do you need to reflect on further?
- How will your practice, and your practice framework, change as a result of your reflections?

CONCEPTUALISATION - *What?*

- What have you learned - can you articulate it clearly and meaningfully?
- What do you want to add to your practice framework?
- What are the unhelpful assumptions that you no longer subscribe to?
- What are the beliefs that you want your work to be based upon?
- What name or label would you give your new practice framework?
- What are the implications of this for this situation?
- What will you do differently if you are in a similar situation again?

COMMITMENT - *Why?*

- Why do you want to make this learning part of your practice?
- Why would it matter if you chose not to change?
- What benefits will the change make for your practice?
- There could be some difficult experiences along the way. Why is it worth withstanding these?
- Who would be least surprised that you want to do this? What do they know about you that leads them to that awareness?
- What skills are you bringing to this change process?
- What do you know about yourself that tells you you're ready and able to do this?

PLANNING

When?

- When will you start to implement your learning?
- When will you monitor progress to ensure your new learning is part of your practice framework?

How?

- How will you put this learning into practice?
- What obstacles or restraints do you anticipate?
- What beliefs could hold you back from doing this?
- What are you afraid will happen if your commitment takes place?
- How do you expect your workplace to respond?
- How could you overcome these obstacles or restraints?
- What one action or decision would free you up to get on with consolidating your new learning?

Where?

- Where will it happen?
- Where can you find the necessary resources?

Who?

- Who will assist or support you in implementing this plan?
- Who could you contract with to support you in embodying the learning?
- Who will provide the feedback you need to help you monitor your progress?

EMBODIMENT

- What are you pleased about?
- What did you do to achieve that?
- What didn't go so well?
- What obstacles, restraints or assumptions got in your way?
- Are you ready to work on these now?

KEY MINI-TOOLS

D. Hewson and M. Carroll *Reflective Supervision Toolkit*

KEY MINI-TOOLS

NON-SUPERVISORY SPACES

CELLAR
Avoidance Space

MANAGER'S OFFICE
Managerial Space

Printed in Great Britain
by Amazon

26627667R00037